CHANGES

The Greatest Poet Alive

Peter Gracey

Simon Peter Music Publishing

This Book of Poem is For You.

CONTENTS

INTRODUCTION

Changes, The Greatest Poet Alive, is a collection of poems capturing the essence of change in all its forms. From the subtle shifts of the ages to the seismic upheavals of our time, this book explores the ways in which change both shapes and challenges us.

In these poems, Peter Gracey invites us to witness the beauty and pain, the joy and sorrow, that change can bring. With a piercing gaze and a compassionate heart, the poet illuminates the truths of our shared human experience, helping us to see ourselves and the world around us in new ways.

Changes is a testament to the power of poetry to transform our understanding of ourselves and the world.

#6

By Peter Gracey

Only the stupid lives with stupidity,
As a man thinketh so is he.
Only the fool will frolic in foolishness,
Five fools you follow,
The sixth your ought to be.

T

AHEAD OF TIME
By Peter Gracey

Suddenly I crawled out of my skin,
understanding who I'm to be,

Suddenly I've hit the chord of life,
suddenly life sings to me.

Ahead of time like it never exist, life feels unfair to me,

When I can experience that,

and you can't experience this.

Crying notes of joy, I'm free.

H

ALL OF A SUDDEN
By Peter Gracey

All of a sudden I felt happier than I was before,
the moment I thought about you.
All of a sudden sadness became more
when I knew he was with you.
All of a sudden I felt so trapped when
there's nothing that I can do.
To break up a lifetime built on so called love,
with a man that loves you too.

All of a sudden I sensed your pain, I know
you could tell that I felt it too,
All of a sudden it felt like rain when
tears come rushing through.
All of a sudden I felt so trapped when
there's nothing that I can do,
To take your hands and seal our lips,
to see what a kiss can do.

All of a sudden I felt happy again, the
moment I knew it was you,
All of a sudden I turned around realizing I was next to you.
All of a sudden I felt so trapped when
there's nothing I can do,
To cease my happiness from an ominous
dream that kept me away from you.

BIRTH

By Peter Gracey

Was it a scary moment or a beautiful world,
When you first opened your eyes at birth?
When the lids pulled back and you first saw light,
Dying from the womb World, to a mortal birth.

E

CHANGES

By Peter Gracey

My God's Love will never change,
Whether you believe it's true or not.
Though only change is the true unchangeable,
And the love of God cannot.

I will walk in an unchanged direction,
To be a part of deity's light.
Cause life is truly unchangeable,
Walking by faith and not by sight.

G

CONTINENT

By Peter Gracey

The Largest continent is the human mind,
Yet we only suffer from our imagination.
Separating the differences between reality and time,
Now time becomes an illusion.

R

DECIDE

By Peter Gracey

Never decide on making someone happy,
Happiness is always about two.
Before you decide to excite someone else,
Make sure its pure ecstasy in you.

Never lie to yourself to please another,
Mere existence is to feel satisfied.
Never decide to make someone happy,
Only within themselves, they will have to decide.

E

DEPRESSED

By Peter Gracey

How does it feel when you've lost your family
and all your so called friends are no more?
How does it feel when you think you're at lowest,
then tomorrow you're even deeper than before?

How do you feel when you're depressed and
panicked, and no one knows your thoughts?
How do you feel when you think of taking
your own life, uncaring about the cost?

How do you feel when your account is in the
negative and waiting for that next check?
How do you feel when you get laid off and
your next is your last check?

Now you've turned around your life
mentoring wealthy men,
How do you feel when you make the same mistakes,
Tumbling back to nothing again?

A

EXPERIENCE
By Peter Gracey

If you want to experience something different,
It's totally up to you.
If you never do something different,
You'll never experience anew.

If you never change the way you think,
You'll be the same old stagnant you.
If you never find your main chief aim,
It's only because of you.

It's very hard to walk away,
From toxic relations too.
But if you make up your mind to take that step,
Your experience will see you through.

T

FEARLESS

By Peter Gracey

Never say "I am only human" placing
limitations on yourself,
Don't the birds and the bees live to their fullest potential?
So why do we do this to ourselves.

As a caged bird may sing and will never fly away if set free,
So are humans who live in their minds
and not imagine what is reality.
We are afraid of things which doesn't exist, and
we live for tomorrow which neither exists.
And it's good intentions why this mess exists.

We all think we are doing things for the right
reasons and not everyone will agree you.
But the unbelievers, also unbelieve for the right reason
and it their good intentions which clashes with you.

Who is right and who is wrong has nothing to do with me,
What you believe and what you stand
for, doesn't set you free.
Free your mind and experience the light,
War will never end in the religous real estate fight.
Experience your thoughts and bloom like a flower,
When you find yourself fearless, take it to the next hour.

FOLLOWING FOOLS

By Peter Gracey

If the five fools who follows,
Feels its fine to follow you.
Do you find yourself as the smartest fool?
Or you find why five fool follows you?

E

FREE (F)

By Peter Gracey

Feeling Free isn't a Far Fetched Feat,

To Find Freedom Focus is First.

Have a Fearless Fixation on Finding yourself,

And Freedom will Find you First.

S

GENTLE SOFTLY SIGH

By Peter Gracey

Gleaming stars light up the sky,
Gentle softly sigh,
Graceful birds take flight and sing,
Gratitude, the joy they bring.

In this world of endless strife,
Let's embrace the gift of life,
With grateful hearts, we'll transcend,
Glorious moments, without end.

T

HELL ON MY SHOULDERS
By Peter Gracey

There's nowhere left to run,
There's nowhere left to hide.
With hell resting on my shoulders,
And heaven standing by my side.

Intentions driving my thoughts,
Habits repeating themselves.
No matter how I think it's hard,
For sure it's harder on someone else.

Now self and the past has become one,
Realizing there's nowhere to run.
The harder the it gets and the more tears I shed,
The more numbing it becomes.

With hell sitting on my shoulders,
And heaven by my side,
I'll walk with faith and not by sight,
With Heaven by my side.

Now faith in what? Is the question,
Burdened with Calvary's cross.
Never knew how to stop running,
Till I brushed my shoulders off.

HOW FAR?
By Peter Gracey

Die in the spiritual world, reborn in the womb world.
Die in the womb world and reborn on earth.
Two things we will never remember,
is the day we open our eyes and the day they're closed;
Guaranteed is death and birth.

P

IMAGINE
By Peter Gracey

What does it mean to express yourself?

What does it mean to imagine?

What does it mean to believe in yourself?

Stop and simply imagine.

O

INESTIMABLE
By Peter Gracey

I don't obey laws,
I create laws,
Cause I am
The most intelligent one.

I don't care for laws,
Naturally I create the laws,
Black is what I am.

E

JAMAICA
By Peter Gracey

Jamaica is on my mind,
Sleeping or awake.
Operating on Jamaica's time,
So sometimes I am late.

To go back to Jamaica,
As my final resting place.
To sleep in harmony with my love,
I'm hopeful that's the case.

T

JOY AND LOVE
By Peter Gracey

You can never find joy in people,
Not in wealth,
Not in health,
Not in the monies,
But only within yourself.

You can never find love in people.
You can only find love within yourself.

Stop searching for joy and love in someone else,
Only they can experience their own.
Live to love and know yourself,
Heaven welcomes you home.

A

LEGACY

By Peter Gracey

Live your legacy now,
Don't wait until you're gone.
We all have the same opportunities,
Think beyond thinking,
It was there before you were born.

Leaving legacies behind,
To me is such a waste of time,
Experiencing my legacy while I'm alive,
Seem much more kind.

L

LIFE
By Peter Gracey

It takes more than one for life to go on,
It would not exist if it was only you.
If there are no one around to experience this so called life,
Then life is pure nothingness and so are you.

We are simply here to experience this thing called life,
And realize there are no such thing as a good or a bad day.
The so called purpose you serve is just
the ambiences of life,
So only you can stand in your way.

You are the control of your world, while
you experience this life,
However you think, you will decide how to feel.
But the way you feel does not determine the quality of life,
It decides what you accept to be false or real.

I

MASTER OF MYSELF
By Peter Gracey

I can only celebrate freedom when I
am the Master of myself,
Spending my days putting the finishing touch on me.
This way I welcome death with my eyes wide open,
Each day I live, each day I'm free.

V

MASTERING MYSELF
By Peter Gracey

Suddenly I have realized that I have past the worst,

Now understanding the importance
of understanding me first.

And to care and to caress and to understand myself,

Controlling my thoughts, to control myself

Knowing "but" is not an option, as confident as can be

Mastering the art of mastering myself

Amen – So mote it be!

E

NECESSITY
By Peter Gracey

We're all here to experience this life,
we're all here to survive.
We're all here to roam this earth
and simply try to stay alive.

No one is surviving any better than you,
Survival simply means to live.
With peace as my basic necessity,
And the courage and the will to live.

Titles and wealth means nothing to me,
I'll Control my intelligence and live.
Old age is the single most blessing,
Grace was meant to give.

A

ON AND ON

By Peter Gracey

Only one thing can end my life, and that's death.
I will keep on creating until my last breath.

I'll keep going on and I'll keep doing me,
And be myself and not what others want me to be.

Never holding on, but keep going on, I'll
keep going on never cease to be.
I'll exhale my breath and fly away free.

G

PAIN AND SUFFERING
By Peter Gracey

Losing a parent is a blessing,
That's the natural order of things.
Losing a child is devastating,
Immense pain and suffering it brings.

E

PRAY OR MEDITATE?
By Peter Gracey

For years we've been dependent on parents,
And some incorporate the trust of priests.
Waiting for years for a savior to come,
While some search for inward peace

Why do we pray or why do we meditate,
A question which separates the inward
and outward mindset of man.
Choose for yourself within or without
Don't be smart as you think you possibly are,
But be as wise as you possibly can.

O

REARRANGE
By Peter Gracey

You cannot step in the same direction twice,
A simple millimeter of change.
You cannot meet the same person twice,
It's a constant rearrange.

F

RUN RUN RUN
By Peter Gracey

Compare yourself to the you of yesterday,
Not who you want to become.
No experience with the you of tomorrow,
You have nowhere to run.
Run, run, run.
You have nowhere to run.
So walk, don't run.
You have nowhere to run.

A

SEARCHING FOR A PURPOSE
By Peter Gracey

Every night I look down at the stars,
Sometimes I think I may be looking up.
Not sure where is up and not sure where is down,
Earth is floating into space, spinning,
round, and round and round.

So when you're looking up, what is it you're looking for?
What if you're looking down, then what is it you're
searching for?
If you're searching for a purpose, know you're only ashes
and dirt to dirt.
Before you look to the heavens, know
you're a product of this earth.

Q

SPACE

By Peter Gracey

I have no power in a space which I have no control,

So now I'll only do intentional things
while mastering my soul.

My mind and the space around me that
I enjoy being by myself,

If you choose to enter my space, know I
am the master and no one else.

So I will lean into my dream which the
universe intended for me,

And by the grace of the creator,

understanding of me.

U

THE PERFECT DAY

By Peter Gracey

I've always thought to myself,
This is the perfect day to die,
The perfect day to give birth,
The perfect day to cry.
The perfect day to win and the perfect day to lose,
God has made a perfect day,
So who am I to choose?

The perfect day to blaspheme,
The perfect day to lie,
I am the perfect of the imperfect,
To fix my imperfections, it's the perfect day to try.

The perfect day to right my wrongs,
And the failures to retry,
The perfect day to lose your wings,
The perfect day to fly.

The perfect day to end, and the perfect day to begin,
The perfect day to love and The perfect day to sin.

The perfect day to take the blame,
The prefect day to accuse,
God has made the perfect day;
Tell me!
Who am I to choose?

TRAPPED

By Peter Gracey

Forget about religion,
Forget about faith.
Forget about love,
Forget about hate.
Forget about the things around you,
Forget about everyone else.
After everyone has used you for their purpose,
There's nothing left but a broken self.

Forget about the show,
Forget about the stage.
Forget about the popularity,
Forget about your age.
Forget about the traps,
Forget about being free.

If I keep trying to be like someone else
Who's trying to be like me?

A

TURIN

By Peter Gracey

Have you ever sensed your~self inside of
you and suddenly life makes sense?

Have you ever seen your~self from inside of
you facing an artificial intelligence?

Brace yourself mankind, the Turin test is done,
your life is about to shatter, the truth is about to come.

The age of Aquarius has shown its face, a new age and a
new order has come,
The age of artificial intelligence and the
age when mankind is done.

R

UNTIL

By Peter Gracey

Until the day I stop thinking and I am no longer aware,
It's the day I'll stop loving you,
And the day after, no one will care.

Until the day I take my last breath,
Clinically no pulse to give.
Until that one day is sure to come,
The remaining days we must live.

Sometimes I close my eyes wishing I was blind,
So not to create more memories of the
loved ones we'll leave behind.

I

SHAKEN BY THOUGHTS
By Peter Gracey

There's always a wrong and a right way,
Whichever you choose, think before you act.
My right way could be your wrong way,
Keep your head up – keep your mind intact.

Artificial as they come,
Be sure to know yourself.
The way you think of another man,
Should be the same of thoughts of yourself.

Either which way you choose,
Just choose to be yourself.
Free to speak and not shaken,
By the thoughts of someone else.

U

WELCOME TO AQUARIUS
By Peter Gracey

Welcome to Aquarius,
Where only our minds can set us free,
Follow the man with the pitcher,
The fishes are no more to be.

The invisible will change in front of our eyes,
Leaving intelligence to sort things out.
The aboriginal intellect that isolates
the smart from the wise,
Now everyone's coming out.

Artificial it may seem,
Now a collective God dictating how man shall live,
Welcome home to Aquarius,
My People, wise up so you can live.

S

PETER GRACEY

YOURSELF

By Peter Gracey

I am responsible for myself,
And where I find myself to be.
No one can help me free myself,
Freeing my mind will set me free.

So I thinketh, so am I,
I am in absolute control of me.
I will not be censored nor owe anyone,
Only freeing my mind will set me free.

PETER GRACEY

Made in the USA
Columbia, SC
15 November 2023

26133766R00028